Drums for Kids

How to Play, Master the Basics and Rock the Rhythm

Table of Contents

Introduction

Have you ever felt a surge of excitement when a powerful drumbeat kicks in on your favorite song? Do you find yourself tapping your feet or drumming on imaginary toms while listening to music? Perhaps you even sneak in some air guitar solos when no one's looking.

If this sounds familiar, then there's a little drummer waiting to burst out of you. So, where do you begin?

There are countless drum books on the market, promising to turn you into a rhythmic maestro. However, many are filled with complex jargon and confusing notation, leaving you frustrated and bewildered.

Drums for Kids is different. It's the perfect starting point for any child who dreams of taking the world by storm with their drumming skills.

Here's why Drums for Kids stands out from the rest:

- **Made for Beginners:** Forget overwhelming theory and complicated exercises. This book starts with the basics: building your drumming foundation brick by brick. You'll learn everything from holding the sticks properly to mastering your first simple beats, all in a clear, concise, and kid-friendly way.

- **Learn by Doing:** Drums for Kids isn't just about reading dry text. It's an interactive experience packed with fun, hands-on activities that will keep you engaged and motivated. Get ready to tap, roll, and fill your way to drumming greatness.

- **Unleash Your Creativity:** Don't just learn to play other people's music. Drums for Kids will nurture your inner rockstar, teaching you how to create your drum compositions and express yourself through rhythm.

- **Endless Musical Styles:** From the heart-pounding beats of rock to the smooth grooves of jazz, this book explores a variety of musical styles. You'll discover how drums add magic to different genres and learn how to incorporate those elements into your drumming.

- **Learn from the Legends:** Take a trip through the fascinating history of drums. Discover how these incredible instruments evolved, and learn about the iconic drummers who have shaped the music we love today.

Drums for Kids is more than just a drumming instruction manual. It's your passport to a universe of rhythmic exploration. Packed with illustrations, helpful tips, and clear explanations, this book will transform you from a silent observer into a rhythmic powerhouse.

Are you ready to turn the drumbeat into your heartbeat?

Prepare to rock the stage!

Chapter 1: Introduction to Drums

A packed stadium roars as the legendary drummer, John Bonham, launches into a heart-stopping solo in Led Zeppelin's "Moby Dick." His powerful strokes pound a relentless rhythm, building a wave of energy that washes over the crowd. The drums become a driving force, a primal call that unites thousands in a shared experience of pure excitement.

1.   Experience the exciting journey of drumming! Source:
https://www.pexels.com/photo/tilt-shift-photo-of-acoustic-drum-
set-995301/

Have you ever wondered what creates those powerful beats, the thundering rhythms that stir something deep within you? The answer lies in the fascinating tradition of drumming... a journey that starts with a simple question. Where did the drum come from, and how did it become a vital part of music across cultures and time?

The Drum as a Percussion Instrument

The drum, that primal force that ignites emotions and drives the beat in countless musical styles, is more than just a hollowed-out log getting pummeled. It's a finely tuned instrument with a rich history, and before you unleash your inner drummer, it's time to discover what makes a drum tick (or rather, thump).

Anatomy of a Drum

Every drum has three essential parts working together to create sound:

- **Drumhead:** This is the beating heart of the drum, a thin, stretched membrane (often called the skin) that vibrates when struck. Made from materials like animal skin, plastic, or mesh, the drumhead's material and thickness significantly impact the sound.

- **Shell:** This is the body of the drum, the sturdy container that holds the drumhead in place. Shells come in a variety of materials, like wood (maple, birch, mahogany), metal (steel, aluminum), or even acrylic, each affecting the drum's resonance and tone.

- **Hoops:** These are the rings that tighten the drumhead onto the shell, acting like a giant tuning fork. By adjusting the tension of the hoops, drummers control the pitch and tone of the drum.

Have you ever wondered how these parts translate a whack from a stick into that powerful beat? Prepare to find out.

How Drums Produce Sound

The magic happens when the drumstick makes contact with the drumhead. The impact causes the drumhead to vibrate rapidly like jelly, trembling after a good shake. This vibration creates waves of sound that travel through the air, reaching your ears as that powerful beat. The drumhead's size, material, and tension all play a role in the sound produced. A larger drumhead vibrates more slowly, resulting in a lower-pitched sound, while a tighter drumhead vibrates faster, creating a higher pitch.

Tuning into the Art of Playing

Just like tightening a guitar string changes its pitch, the tension of the drumhead affects the sound it produces. Drummers use tuning lugs, the little bolts around the hoop, to adjust the tension and achieve the desired pitch for different beats. A tighter head produces a higher-pitched "crack" sound, while a looser head produces a lower-pitched "boom" sound. This ability to manipulate the pitch through tuning allows drummers to create a wide range of sounds and tonal variations.

Beyond the Basic Beat

There's more to drumming than just hitting the drum. Drummers learn various techniques to create different sounds and rhythms, transforming simple strikes into complex patterns. Some fundamental techniques include:

- **Single Strokes:** These are the building blocks of drumming: one clean hit on the drumhead with each hand. Mastering single strokes ensures precise control and lays the foundation for more complex techniques.

- **Rolls:** Drummers achieve a continuous stream of sound by rapidly alternating strokes on the drumhead, creating a smooth, flowing melody. There are different types of rolls, each with its unique sound and feel.

- **Flams:** This technique involves playing two closely spaced strokes very quickly, creating a "double tap" sound. It adds a distinctive accent to a beat and takes some practice to master.

These are just a taste of the many drumming techniques waiting to be explored. As your drumming skills evolve, you'll discover countless creative ways to express yourself through rhythm, from intricate fills to thunderous grooves.

The Musical Significance of the Drum

The drum isn't just a supporting instrument in the background. It's the very foundation upon which most music is built. It's the rhythmic heartbeat that drives the melody forward, creating the groove that makes you want to tap your foot or move your body. It's time to dive deeper into the magic drums bring to music:

The Foundation of Rhythm

- **The Pulse of the Song:** Drums act as the timekeeper, providing the steady pulse that anchors the entire piece. They lay down the beat, a rhythmic framework that all other instruments and vocals follow.

- **Building the Groove:** A groove is that infectious feeling that makes you want to move. In collaboration with the bassist, drummers create the groove by locking into a tight rhythmic interplay. The drum and bass parts fit together seamlessly, creating a foundation upon which other instruments can build.

- **Dynamic Duos:** Drummers often have a special connection with the bassist. They work together to create a strong rhythmic foundation, pushing and pulling the tempo, adding accents, and building tension and release throughout the song.

2. *The dynamic duo: drummer and bassist. Source: https://www.pexels.com/photo/man-in-black-crew-neck-shirt-playing-drums-near-a-man-playing-guitar-7503241/*

Drumming Styles and Genres

Just like different languages have unique accents and pronunciations, drumming styles have their distinct flavors. Here's a glimpse into some popular styles:

- **Rock:** Rock drumming is known for its powerful beats and driving rhythms. Rock drummers often combine single strokes, double strokes, and fills to create energy and excitement.

- **Jazz:** Jazz drumming is all about improvisation and creating a dynamic, ever-evolving groove. Jazz drummers are masters of using brushes, cymbals, and intricate techniques to create a sophisticated and nuanced sound.

- **World Music:** From Africa's complex polyrhythms to Japan's thunderous taiko drums, world music offers a vast array of drumming styles. Each culture has its unique way of using drums, reflecting their musical traditions and storytelling through rhythm.

Every style utilizes different techniques and emphasizes specific aspects of the drum set. A rock drummer might focus on powerful bass drum kicks and crashing cymbals, while a jazz drummer might focus on delicate cymbal work and intricate snare rolls.

Evolution of Drum Sets

The modern drum set, with its array of drums, cymbals, and stands, is a product of a long and fascinating history. Here's a quick look at its evolution:

- **Humble Beginnings:** Early drum sets were simple setups, often consisting of a snare drum, a bass drum, and maybe a cymbal or two. These setups were used in marching bands and early forms of popular music.

- **The Rise of Jazz:** In the early 20th century, the rise of jazz music spurred the development of more complex drum sets. Drummers needed more options to create the dynamic and expressive rhythms demanded by the genre.

- **The Rock Revolution:** The arrival of rock and roll in the 1950s pushed the boundaries of drumming even further. Drummers like John Bonham and Keith Moon incorporated multiple toms, additional cymbals, and powerful double bass drumming techniques, creating the foundation for the modern rock sound.

- **Global Inspiration:** Throughout history, drummers have been influenced by music from around the world. The incorporation of instruments like congas and bongos from Latin music or djembes from Africa has further expanded the drum set's sonic palette.

The journey of the drum set doesn't end there. As music continues to evolve, drummers will undoubtedly find new ways to push the boundaries of their instrument, creating even more exciting and innovative ways to drive the music forward.

The Cultural Significance of the Drum

Drums are cultural cornerstones woven into the fabric of societies worldwide. From the heart-pounding rhythms of

West Africa to the intricate beats of India, drums have been a powerful force for centuries.

Drums Across the Globe

Take a musical journey around the world, and you'll encounter a diverse array of drums, each with its own unique sound and cultural significance:

- **The Djembe:** This goblet-shaped drum, hailing from West Africa, is known for its deep, resonant bass and bright, slapping highs. It's a vital part of traditional music and ceremonies, often used for celebratory gatherings, storytelling, and even religious rituals.

- **The Conga:** This Cuban powerhouse comes in various sizes and produces a wide range of tones, from sharp slaps to deep, rich grooves. Congas are the backbone of Latin music genres like salsa and rumba, adding an upbeat energy to the rhythm section.

- **The Tabla:** A pair of intricately carved hand drums from India, the tabla produces complex, layered sounds. It is a cornerstone of Hindustani classical music, used for both rhythmic accompaniment and intricate solos that showcase the skill of the player.

- **The Taiko Drum:** The thunderous boom of Japanese Taiko drums in a festival procession is unforgettable. These massive drums, with their deep, resonating sound, are a powerful symbol of Japanese culture and tradition. Often played in large ensembles, Taiko drums create a captivating spectacle of rhythm and energy.

- **The Capoeira Berimbau:** Take a trip to Brazil and immerse yourself in the mesmerizing polyrhythms of Capoeira rodas, a martial art form that blends dance, acrobatics, and music. The berimbau, a unique single-stringed instrument played with a stick and a gourd, is the heart of the Capoeira rhythm section. Its buzzing tones and rhythmic variations provide the foundation for the improvisational movements of the Capoeira players.

- **The Pow Wow Drum:** Journey to the Americas and experience the haunting melodies coaxed from the Native American Pow Wow drum. These large, hand-held drums create a steady beat that forms the backbone of Pow Wow music, an electrifying celebration of Native American culture and heritage. The hypnotic rhythm of the Pow Wow drum is a powerful connection to the land and the ancestors.

3. The Pow Wow Drum. Source: Frank Kovalchek from Anchorage, Alaska, USA, CC BY 2.0 <https://creativecommons.org/licenses/by/2.0>, via Wikimedia Commons. https://commons.wikimedia.org/wiki/File:Musical_instruments_on_display_at_the_MIM_(14348462211).jpg

These are just a few examples. Drums come in countless shapes, sizes, and materials worldwide, each reflecting the unique cultural traditions where they originated. Whether it's the thunderous boom of Japanese Taiko drums in a festival procession, the mesmerizing polyrhythms of Brazilian Capoeira rodas, or the haunting melodies coaxed from a Native American Pow Wow drum, the global language of drumming transcends spoken languages, uniting people through rhythm.

Drums in Rituals and Communication

The history of drums goes far beyond musical accompaniment. For centuries, drums have been a powerful tool for communication and ceremony:

- **Drumbeats as Messages:** In some African cultures, drummers developed intricate rhythms to convey messages over long distances. These "talking drums" could announce births, deaths, or even warnings of danger, functioning as a vital communication network. Long ago, a complex rhythm echoed across the savanna, carrying news from village to village with incredible speed and accuracy.

- **Signaling Events:** Drums have played a crucial role in marking important events throughout history. From battle cries of rallying warriors to ceremonial rhythms accompanying religious festivals, drumbeats are a powerful way to signal and commemorate significant occasions. Picture the booming war drums sending chills down the spines of opposing armies or the celebratory frenzy ignited by joyous festival rhythms.

The Spiritual Connection

In many cultures, drums hold a deeper significance, a connection to the spiritual world.

- **Drumming as Expression:** The rhythmic act of drumming is a form of spiritual expression, a way to connect with inner feelings and emotions. The powerful pulse of the drum is cathartic, allowing participants to release tension and connect with their primal selves. In a group drumming ceremony, participants lose themselves in the rhythm, expressing emotions that words cannot capture.

- **Meditation in Motion:** In some cultures, drumming is used as a form of meditation, focusing the mind and achieving a state of inner peace. The repetitive rhythm is hypnotic, creating a sense of calmness and clarity. Picture a lone drummer, eyes closed, using a steady beat to enter a meditative state.

- **Connecting with the Divine:** Drums are a bridge between the human and the divine. In certain religious traditions, drumming is used to invoke deities, create a sacred space, or accompany prayers and chants. The resonant boom of drums echoing through a temple creates a powerful connection between the earthly and the spiritual realms.

The drum is a portal to a universe of rhythm, history, and cultural expression. From the intricate techniques used by modern drummers to the ancient traditions of using drums for communication and spiritual connection, drums have been a powerful force for millennia.

You've explored the diverse sounds of drums across the globe, from the thunderous boom of the Taiko drum to the mesmerizing polyrhythms of the Capoeira berimbau. You've learned how drumbeats transcended spoken language, carried messages, signaled events, and connected people to their cultural roots. You've also dipped your toes into the spiritual significance of drumming as a form of expression, meditation, and a bridge to the divine.

So, if you've ever felt the primal urge to tap your foot or pound on a table in rhythm, there's a reason for it. Your drum set awaits, brimming with exciting possibilities. With dedication and practice, you, too, can unlock the power of rhythm and become part of this tradition.

Embrace the beat and unleash your inner drummer.

Chapter 2: Getting Started with the Drum

The beat is calling, and you're ready to answer. However, before you launch into a thunderous solo, you must explore the essentials of starting your drumming journey. This chapter is your roadmap to selecting the perfect drum set and understanding the key components that make it thump. Prepare to transform from a curious observer to a budding drummer poised to conquer the beat.

4. Get ready to play the drums professionally. Source:
https://www.pexels.com/photo/girl-having-fun-playing-bass-
drum-9644679/

Selecting the Right Drum and Equipment

Once you're fired up to explore the nuances of drumming, it's time to choose your first drum set and essential equipment.

Complete vs. Piecemeal Drum Sets

As a drumming newbie, you might be wondering if you should jump straight into buying individual drums or opt for a complete set. Here's a quick breakdown:

- **Complete Drum Sets:** These pre-configured packages include all the essential drums (snare, bass drum, toms, cymbals) and sometimes even a hardware stand to hold everything together. They're a great starting point, especially for acoustic drums, as they ensure compatibility and provide everything you need to begin drumming right away. Plus, complete sets often come at a more affordable price point compared to buying individual components.

- **Piecemeal Kits:** For experienced drummers or those with specific preferences, buying individual drums and hardware allows for customization. You can mix and match components from different brands or upgrade specific pieces as your skills progress. However, for beginners, navigating compatibility and choosing the right pieces is overwhelming. It's also important to factor in the additional cost of purchasing hardware stands separately.

Choosing Your First Drum Set (Acoustic or Electronic)

Acoustic and electronic drums have pros and cons, and the best choice depends on your budget, living situation, and drumming goals. Consider consulting a friendly drum shop staff member. They will answer your questions and guide you toward the perfect set based on your needs and aspirations.

- **Acoustic Drums:** This is the classic choice, offering a natural playing experience and the rich, full sound that defines drumming. Nothing beats the feeling of hitting a real drumhead and the raw energy it creates. However, they require dedicated practice space and are quite loud, potentially causing noise complaints from neighbors or roommates. Apartment dwellers or those with limited space might find acoustic drums impractical.

- **Electronic Drums:** A more modern option, electronic drum sets are compact and much quieter, perfect for apartment living or late-night practice sessions. They often come with built-in practice features like headphone jacks and backing tracks, making them ideal for learning without disturbing anyone. Additionally, some electronic sets offer the ability to adjust volume and even switch between different drum sounds, allowing you to explore a wider range of musical styles. However, the playing experience might feel different due to the electronic pads instead of traditional drumheads. The rebound and feel of electronic pads can take some getting used to for drummers accustomed to acoustic kits.

5. Electronic drums. Source: https://www.pexels.com/photo/black-and-red-remote-control-on-black-tablet-computer-4090902/

Essential Drumming Accessories

Once you have your set, you'll need a few key accessories to complete your drumming arsenal:

- **Drumsticks:** These are your tools of the trade. They come in various materials (wood, nylon) and sizes, so experiment to find the pair that feels right for your hand size and playing style. Lighter sticks are good for beginners as they require less effort to swing, while heavier sticks offer more power and control for experienced players.

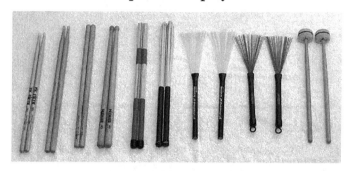

6. *Different kinds of drumsticks. Source: Andrewa, CC BY-SA 3.0 <https://creativecommons.org/licenses/by-sa/3.0>, via Wikimedia Commons. https://commons.wikimedia.org/wiki/File:Drum_sticks.jpg*

- **Throne (Drum Seat):** Comfort is key. A good drum throne provides proper posture and support for extended practice sessions. Look for a throne with adjustable height to ensure correct positioning behind the drum set.

- **Practice Pad:** This portable pad allows you to silently warm up your drumming muscles or practice rudiments (basic drumming patterns) without disturbing anyone. Practice pads come in various sizes and materials, offering different playing experiences. A rubber pad is quiet for late-night practice, while a mesh pad can provide a more realistic feel closer to a real drumhead.

7. *Practice Pad. Source: Vladimir Morozov from Russia, CC BY 2.0 <https://creativecommons.org/licenses/by/2.0>, via Wikimedia Commons. https://commons.wikimedia.org/wiki/File:Practice_pad_-_Vladimir_Morozov.jpg*

Beyond the essentials, some optional accessories can enhance your drumming experience:

- **Headphones (for Electronic Drums):** These allow for private practice without disturbing others, especially useful for late-night sessions.

- **Metronome:** This handy tool helps you develop a solid sense of timing, a crucial skill for any drummer. A metronome provides a steady click track that you can practice playing along to, ensuring your beats are tight and consistent. Many electronic drum sets have built-in metronomes, but a dedicated metronome can offer more features and customization options.

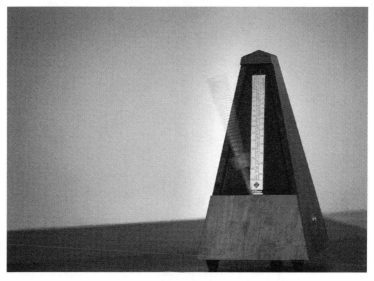

8. *Metronome. Source: https://www.pexels.com/photo/close-up-of-a-moving-metronome-7220729/*

- **Drum Rug:** This helps keep your drum set in place and protects your floor from scratches and scuffs.

- **Drumstick Holder:** This keeps your drumsticks within easy reach while you're playing.

- **Ear Protection:** If you're practicing with acoustic drums for extended periods, especially with headphones (which can block out some ambient noise), it's a good idea to wear ear protection to safeguard your hearing.

The Drum Set Layout

After you've chosen your gear, it's time to get familiar with the layout of your drum set. It's your command center of rhythm, where each component plays a specific role in creating powerful beats.

Here are the key players in your drumming ensemble:

- **The Bass Drum:** The backbone of the beat, this large drum sits on the floor and is played with your dominant foot by using a pedal. The bass drum provides the low-end thump that drives the groove.

9.   The Bass Drum. Source: Leanne, CC BY 2.0 <https://creativecommons.org/licenses/by/2.0>, via Wikimedia Commons. https://commons.wikimedia.org/wiki/File:Bass_drum_Premier_(8639408589).jpg

- **The Snare Drum:** This is the workhorse of the drum set, responsible for the crisp, cracking sound that defines many drumbeats. It's typically positioned slightly to the left of the bass drum and played with your non-dominant hand.

10. The Snare Drum. Source: Vladimir Morozov from Russia, CC BY 2.0 <https://creativecommons.org/licenses/by/2.0>, via Wikimedia Commons. https://commons.wikimedia.org/wiki/File:Snare_drum_-_Vladimir_Morozov.jpg

- **Tom Toms (Toms):** These are the higher-pitched drums of the set, typically coming in pairs (two toms) or triplets (three toms). They are arranged in a tiered fashion to your right, with the smallest tom positioned highest and the largest tom positioned lowest. Toms add tonal variations and accents to your drumming.

*11. Tom Toms. Source: Andrewa, CC BY-SA 4.0
<https://creativecommons.org/licenses/by-sa/4.0>, via Wikimedia
Commons.
https://commons.wikimedia.org/wiki/File:Hanging_tom_double_
mount.png*

- **The Hi-Hat Cymbal:** This versatile cymbal consists of two cymbals mounted on a stand that is opened and closed with a foot pedal. You can play the hi-hat with both your foot (closed hi-hat sound) and your stick (open hi-hat sound) to create a variety of rhythmic patterns. The hi-hat often keeps the time and provides accents in between snare hits.

12. The Hi-Hat Cymbal. Source: Subdivision by zero, CC BY-SA 4.0 <https://creativecommons.org/licenses/by-sa/4.0>, via Wikimedia Commons. https://commons.wikimedia.org/wiki/File:Zildjian_Quick_Beat_H i_Hat_15.jpg

- **Crash Cymbal(s):** These cymbals add punctuation and emphasis to your drumming. They are typically positioned above the toms and are struck with your stick for explosive crashes that accentuate specific moments in the music. The number of crash cymbals varies depending on the drum set, with some drummers opting for one crash cymbal while others might have two or even more.

*13. Crash Cymbal. Source: Orion Cymbals, CC BY-SA 3.0
<https://creativecommons.org/licenses/by-sa/3.0>, via Wikimedia
Commons.
https://commons.wikimedia.org/wiki/File:Mainstream_thin_cras
h_orion.png*

This is just a basic layout, and the arrangement of your drum set should be customized to your playing style and preferences. The important thing is to find a configuration that feels comfortable and allows you to reach all the components easily. As you gain drumming experience, you might explore adding additional cymbals or even different types of drums to expand your sonic palette.

A Deeper Look Inside the Drum

In Chapter 1, you explored the core components of a drum, including the drumhead, shell, and hoops. Now, it's time to take a closer look at these essential parts and how they work together to create the sound you love.

- **Drumhead:** This is the heart of the drum, the thin membrane that vibrates when struck. Drumheads come in various materials like animal skin (calfskin), plastic, or mesh, each affecting the sound in unique ways. However, did you know there are two drumheads on most drums?

14. *Drumhead. Source: Bikinibomb, Public domain, via Wikimedia Commons.*
https://commons.wikimedia.org/wiki/File:Drumhead.jpg

- **Batter Head:** This is the head that gets struck by the drumstick and plays the most significant role in the sound you hear. Batter heads come in different thicknesses and materials, with thicker heads producing a lower pitch and thinner heads producing a higher pitch. The drummer can also adjust the tension of the batter head using the tuning lugs around the hoop. A tighter batter head produces a higher-pitched sound with more attack, while a looser head produces a lower-pitched sound with more resonance.

- **Resonant Head (or Resonant Drumhead):** This is the head on the underside of the drum. It doesn't get struck directly but vibrates in sympathy with the batter head, affecting the overall tone and sustain of the drum. Resonant heads are usually thinner than batter heads and can also be muffled using dampeners to control the amount of resonance. The interplay between the batter head and the resonant head significantly impacts the sound of the drum.

By experimenting with different types of drumheads and tuning them appropriately, you can achieve a wide range of sounds from your drums, shaping them to fit your desired musical style. It's a crucial part of a drummer's journey to crafting their unique sound.

An Anatomy of Drumsticks

After you're familiar with the drum set layout, turn your attention to the essential tools you'll wield to create those driving beats. Your drumsticks are simple implements that come in various shapes and sizes, each affecting the sound you produce and your overall playing experience.

The Key Components

A drumstick can be broken down into three main parts:

- **The Butt:** This is the thicker end of the stick that you grip with your hand. It provides leverage and control as you strike the drum. The butt can be made from the same material as the shaft, or it can be capped with a rubber or nylon tip for added durability and comfort.

- **The Shaft:** This is the main body of the stick, the long, slender section that connects the butt to the tip. Shafts are typically made of wood or plastic, with wood being the more traditional choice. The shaft's material and thickness affect the stick's weight, balance, and rebound. Thicker shafts offer more power for heavier hitting, while thinner shafts provide more flexibility and speed for faster playing. Wield a thick oak shaft for powerful rock drumming or opt for a lighter maple shaft for intricate jazz fills.

- **The Tip:** This is the pointed end of the stick that makes contact with the drumhead. The tip material (wood, nylon, plastic) and shape (round, acorn, barrel) influence the sound you produce. Wooden tips produce a warmer sound, while nylon or plastic tips offer a brighter attack. The shape of the tip also affects the sound. A round tip provides a more focused sound, ideal for precise cymbal work, while an acorn or barrel tip offers a larger contact area for a fuller sound on the drumhead.

Tip

Shoulder

Shaft

Butt

15. The main parts of a drumstick. Source: en:User:Lupin, User:Stannered, Public domain, via Wikimedia Commons. https://commons.wikimedia.org/wiki/File:Drumstick_anatomy.sv g

Material Matters

Drumsticks come in two main materials: wood and plastic. Here's a quick breakdown:

- **Wood:** This is the traditional choice, offering a natural feel and response. Wood comes in various types, each with its sonic characteristics. Hickory is the most popular choice for its durability and versatility. Maple offers a lighter weight and a faster rebound, which is ideal for fast passages or intricate drumming styles. At the same time, oak provides more power and a heavier feel, perfect for laying down a solid backbeat in rock or metal music.

- **Plastic:** A more durable and affordable option, particularly for beginners, plastic sticks are less prone to breaking and are a good choice for practicing rudiments or on electronic drums. However, they may not offer the same warmth, responsiveness, and subtle nuances in sound compared to wooden sticks.

Weight and the Power Factor

The weight of a drumstick, determined by its material and thickness, plays a significant role in the sound and power of your drumming. Here's a general guideline:

- **Lighter Sticks:** These offer faster speed and better rebound, ideal for intricate drumming or lighter musical styles like jazz or funk. They allow for quick movement around the drum set and facilitate complex patterns.

- **Heavier Sticks:** These provide more power and punch for heavier-hitting styles like rock or metal. Heavier sticks help deliver a strong backbeat and allow you to hit harder without sacrificing control.

Choosing the right drumstick ultimately depends on your playing style, musical preference, and personal comfort. Experiment with different materials, weights, and tip shapes to find the perfect pair that allows you to express yourself musically. In the next chapter, you'll explore basic yet exciting drumming techniques, where you'll put your newfound knowledge of drumsticks and drum set layout to work, creating your first rhythmic expressions.

Chapter 3: Drum Playing Techniques

Ever wonder how your favorite drummers lay down those infectious beats? It all boils down to solid technique. This chapter is your guide to becoming a drumming machine. You'll learn essential skills like stick grip, posture, and stroke control, transforming your wild flailing arms into a powerhouse of rhythm. Get ready to impress your friends and maybe even annoy your neighbors a little, so grab your sticks, sit up straight, and unlock your inner drumming genius.

16. Drumming is all about technique. Source:
https://www.pexels.com/photo/cute-kid-playing-drums-7714293/

Holding the Sticks

The foundation of your drumming journey starts with how you hold the sticks. The most popular and versatile grip for beginners is called the matched grip.

Here's how to master it:

- **Hold Gently:** Your fingers should curve around the stick with a light touch, allowing for natural movement and control. This relaxed grip will help you play faster fills and quieter passages with ease.

- **Thumbs Up (for Light Guidance):** Place your thumb on the top of the stick, near the middle, for gentle guidance. It's there to provide subtle support, not to squeeze the life out of the stick. Let your thumb be a balancing weight, working in harmony with your relaxed fingers.

- **Loosen Up for Power:** A relaxed grip might feel counterintuitive at first, but it allows for more control and power. Tightening your grip will make you tense and limit your dexterity. You should be able to bounce the stick gently in your hand. This looser grip will help you avoid fatigue and tension as you play longer.

The matched grip is your best friend as you start. It provides a solid foundation that will translate well to any other grip you might want to explore later. Once you're comfortable with the matched grip and have a basic understanding of drumming fundamentals, feel free to experiment with other options to find what complements your drumming style.

Posture for Power and Precision

A drummer hunched over their kit and flailing their arms wildly is not exactly a recipe for rhythmic mastery, right? Good posture is the secret weapon of every great drummer. It provides a solid foundation for power and comfort and, most importantly, prevents injuries. Here's how to sit like a drumming pro:

- **Spine Up, Shoulders Back:** Imagine a string pulling your head straight up toward the ceiling. Maintain a natural curve in your lower back, with your shoulders relaxed and pulled back. This posture ensures your core is engaged, providing stability and allowing you to transfer power from your body to your strokes.

- **Feet Planted, Hips Stacked:** Sit with your feet flat on the floor, hip-width apart. This creates a stable base and allows you to adjust your position around the kit easily. Avoid crossing your legs, as this restricts your movement and throws off your balance.

Wrist Work

Once you're sitting tall, pay attention to your hand position. Forget about swinging your arms like a windmill. The key to controlled and powerful strokes lies in your wrists.

- **Hands Aloft:** Let your hands hover slightly above the drums, with your fingers relaxed and curved. This creates a natural space for your wrists to move freely and generate powerful yet controlled strokes.

- **The Wrist Whisperer:** Focus on using small, precise wrist movements. Your arms should primarily be there for support, not to generate the force behind each hit. This technique will improve your speed and accuracy and prevent you from tiring out quickly.

- **Elbows In:** Keep your elbows relaxed and close to your body. This helps maintain proper wrist alignment and prevents tension in your shoulders.

By mastering good posture and focusing on wrist motion, you'll be well on your way to becoming a drumming machine with power, precision, and, most importantly, a healthy playing style.

Stroke Techniques, Different Grips, and Stick Control

After you get comfortable with your drum set and drumsticks, it's time to discover the essential techniques to transform them into an instrument of rhythmic expression. Mastering these techniques takes time and dedication, but with consistent practice, you'll be laying down powerful beats in no time.

Single Stroke

The single stroke is the cornerstone of all drumming. It's the basic building block upon which all other techniques are built. Mastering the single stroke will ensure clean, controlled hits and lay the foundation for your drumming journey.

Here's how to execute a single stroke:

1. **Grip and Posture:** Hold your sticks with a relaxed grip. Sit up straight with good posture, with your back straight and your shoulders relaxed.

2. **The Motion:** Let your arm move up and down like a piston in an engine. Raise one stick comfortably above the drum (snare drum for this example).

3. **The Downward Strike:** Focus on using your wrist to bring the stick down and strike the drumhead with the tip. Aim for the center of the drumhead for a clear sound.

4. **Follow Through:** After striking the drum, don't clamp up. Let your arm and wrist follow through naturally in a smooth upward motion. The stick should rebound slightly off the drumhead.

Key Points

- Maintain a relaxed grip throughout the stroke. Tightness will hinder your control and speed.

- Focus on smooth, controlled movements. Avoid jerky motions.

- Follow through with the stroke for a clean sound and a proper rebound.

Practice Tip: Start slow and focus on accuracy. Gradually increase your speed as your control improves. Use a metronome (electronic device that clicks at a steady tempo) to practice keeping time with your single strokes.

Double Stroke

The double stroke is a variation in which the stick rebounds twice on the drumhead with a single downward motion. It creates a faster, more rolling sound than a single stroke.

Mastering the Basics First: Before attempting double strokes, it's crucial to have a solid foundation in single strokes.

Ensure you can play clean and controlled single strokes at various tempos.

Here's a breakdown of the double stroke:

1. **Start with a Single Stroke:** Begin with the single stroke motion, raising the stick and striking the drumhead with a controlled downward motion.

2. **The Bounce:** As the stick rebounds off the drumhead after the initial hit, use controlled finger movement to allow it to bounce lightly on the drumhead a second time.

3. **Follow Through:** After the second hit, follow through with the upward motion as you would in a single stroke.

The double stroke should feel like a natural extension of the single stroke, with the focus being on controlling the stick's rebound for the second hit.

Sticking Techniques

Sticking refers to the sequence in which your hands hit the drums. Understanding basic sticking techniques is essential for playing coordinated beats.

Many fundamental beats utilize alternating sticking, where you hit the drums with alternating hands (Right hand, Left hand, Right hand, Left hand, and so on). This is often abbreviated as RLRL.

Here are 3 common sticking techniques:

- **RLRL (Alternating):** This is the most fundamental sticking and the foundation for many basic beats.

- **RRLL (Double Right Hand Lead):** This emphasizes the right hand for a stronger attack, often used in fills or accents.

- **LLRR (Double Left Hand Lead):** This is similar to RRLL but with a focus on the left hand for a different feel.

Practice Tip: Use a metronome and practice playing single strokes with different sticking patterns (RLRL, RRLL, LLRR) to get comfortable with coordinating your hands.

Rudiments

Drum rudiments are short, repetitive drum patterns that are the building blocks of more complex drumming. Mastering these basic patterns will improve your dexterity, speed, and coordination.

Some essential rudiments include:

- **Single Stroke Roll:** A continuous stream of single strokes played with alternating hands.

- **Double Stroke Roll:** A continuous stream of double strokes played with alternating hands.

- **Paradiddle:** This is a rudiment that alternates between single strokes and double strokes. As you gather skills and experience, explore many other essential rudiments. These rudiments provide a rich vocabulary that you can use to create your unique drumming style.

Stick Control

Developing good stick control is crucial for becoming a well-rounded drummer. It allows you to play with accuracy, power, and dynamics (volume variation). Stick control is heavily influenced by your grip.

Gripping Techniques

While the matched grip is fantastic for beginners, there are a whole lot of drumming styles that utilize different grips. These alternative grips will unlock unique sounds, playing styles, and feels. Here are a few to pique your interest:

- **Traditional Grip:** This grip flips one hand over, creating an asymmetrical style often used in jazz drumming. It offers a looser feel and is helpful for intricate hi-hat work.

- **German Grip:** This is similar to the traditional grip but with the thumb underneath the stick for more power. This grip is popular with some metal and hard rock drummers.

- **French Grip (Pinched Grip):** The stick rests between the thumb and the side of your index finger, offering a unique rebound and sound. This grip is known for its quiet playing style and its usefulness for delicate passages.

- **Moeller Technique:** This grip focuses on finger control for quiet, dynamic playing. It's handy for intricate snare drum work and ghost notes.

- **Push-Pull Technique:** This technique utilizes a combination of pushing and pulling motions for efficient and powerful strokes. This grip is often used by heavy hitters who need to lay down a solid foundation.

Experiment with different grips to find one that feels comfortable and allows you to have good control over the sticks. The grip is a personal preference, and there's no single "correct" way to hold the sticks. The most important factor is finding a grip that enables you to play comfortably and accurately.

Practice on a Pad

Before moving to the drum set, it's highly beneficial to practice your strokes and develop stick control on a practice pad. A practice pad is a small rubber pad mounted on a stand that provides a quiet surface to hone your drumming skills.

Here's why practicing on a pad is so effective:

- **It Reduces Noise:** This allows you to practice at any hour without disturbing others.

- **It Focuses on Technique:** Without the distraction of the full drum set, you can concentrate solely on your grip, stroke mechanics, and developing proper muscle memory.

- **It Builds Stamina:** Practicing on a pad will strengthen the muscles in your wrists and arms, improving your endurance for longer drumming sessions.

Practice Tips

- Start using a metronome and practice single and double strokes on the pad, focusing on clean contact, spacing, and controlled motion.

- Once comfortable, experiment with different sticking patterns (RLRL, RRLL, LLRR) on the pad.

- Gradually incorporate rudiments into your practice routine. Many rudiment exercises can be effectively practiced on a pad.

As you develop good stick control on the practice pad, you can then transfer those skills to the drum set, allowing you to play with greater accuracy, power, and finesse. This chapter has equipped you with the fundamental techniques to navigate the drum set with confidence. The more you play, the more comfortable and precise your movements will become. Experiment with different strokes and grips to find what works best for you. With dedication and these essential techniques under your belt, you'll be laying down killer beats in no time.

Chapter 4: Building Drum Skills

As a teen drummer, you're probably itching to lay down some killer beats. However, before you go all John Bonham on your kit, it's essential to master the fundamental strokes and simple melodies. Don't worry... this isn't boring. It's the foundation for creating awesome grooves. This chapter dives into essential practice strategies and guides you through your first steps in creating simple melodies on the drum set.

17. it's essential to master the fundamental strokes and simple melodies. Source: https://www.pexels.com/photo/a-teenager-plays-the-drum-10738145/

Practice Strategies and Simple Melodies

Equipped with the foundational techniques of drumming, it's time to put them into action:

Effective Practice Strategies

- **Start Slow and Focus on Accuracy:** Don't rush. It's more important to play exercises and rudiments slowly and accurately than to speed through them

---

with mistakes. As your control improves, gradually increase the tempo.

- **Use a Metronome:** Your drumming experience will be much smoother with a trusty metronome by your side. This electronic device provides a steady click track that helps you develop a solid sense of timing, a crucial skill for any drummer. Practice playing single strokes, double strokes, and rudiments along with the metronome to internalize a consistent tempo.

- **Record Yourself:** Technology is your friend. Record yourself playing exercises or simple beats on your phone or any recording device. Listening back allows you to identify areas for improvement and track your progress over time.

- **Make It Fun:** Drumming should be enjoyable. To keep things interesting, incorporate different exercises and styles of music into your practice routine. Play along with your favorite songs (use headphones if necessary), or explore online resources for beginner-friendly drum grooves.

- **Warm Up and Cool Down:** Just like any physical activity, it's important to warm up your muscles before drumming and cool down afterward. Simple stretches for your arms, wrists, and shoulders will help prevent injuries.

Creating Simple Drum Beats

Prepare to turn those basic hits and hand movements you learned into short drum patterns. Here are some steps to get you started:

1. **Play a Basic Rhythm:** Start by tapping out a steady beat on the snare drum with your hands, hitting it twice (RL), and then switching hands (LR). Try to do this slowly at first, and keep going at a steady pace like a ticking clock.

2. **Add a Hi-Hat:** The hi-hat cymbal (usually played with your foot) can add a ticking sound in between your snare hits. Try tapping your foot on the pedal fast to make a swish-swish-swish sound (closed hi-hat) along with your snare drum beat.

3. **Kick It with the Bass Drum:** The bass drum (played with your other foot) adds a deep thump to the beat. Try stomping your foot on the pedal once on the first beat (like a heartbeat) and again on the third beat (one-two-three-four), along with your snare and hi-hat.

4. **Mix It Up:** Now that you have this basic pattern going, try changing things up a bit. Play the snare drum with just your right hand a few times (RR) in between your regular snare hits. Or, try hitting a cymbal with your stick once on the first beat (like a crash). Experiment and see what sounds cool to you.

These are just starting points. The beauty of drumming lies in its creativity. As you develop your skills, explore different beat variations, experiment with sticking patterns, and incorporate fills (short bursts of drumming) to create your unique rhythmic expressions.

Practice makes progress. With dedication and consistent practice, you'll transform these basic techniques into a powerful tool for musical expression.

Demystifying Drum Notation

Once you've grasped the essential techniques and created your first basic beats, it's time to understand drum notation, the language that translates rhythmic ideas onto the page. Just like sheet music for other instruments, drum notation provides a blueprint for the drummer, outlining the specific notes (drum hits) and patterns to be played.

The Staff

In drum notation, the staff is a set of five horizontal lines and four spaces between them. Each line and space has a designated number, ranging from staff line 0 (the top line) to staff line 8 (the bottom line). Reading drum music follows the same principle as reading a book, from left to right and top to bottom. The staff is your roadmap, guiding you through the rhythmic landscape of the music.

Time Signatures

Drum music, like most other music, utilizes time signatures to specify the number of beats per measure and the type of note that gets one beat. A common time signature in drum music is 4/4, which means there are four beats per measure, and each quarter note gets one beat.

Decoding the Drum Symbols

Now that you know the lay of the land (the staff), it's time to decipher the symbols that represent the different drums and cymbals in your drum set. These symbols, placed on specific lines or spaces of the staff, tell you exactly which drum to hit and when. Here's a breakdown of the basic drum symbols, starting from the bottom of the staff:

- **The Bass Drum:** The mighty bass drum, often the foundation of the beat, is typically represented by a dot with a stem pointing upward. This symbol usually sits on the lowest space (staff line 7) of the staff.

- **The Floor Tom:** Moving up the staff, the floor tom or low tom is often depicted by a similar dot with a stem positioned on the second space from the bottom (staff line 5).

- **The Snare Drum:** The ever-important snare drum, the workhorse of the kit, also uses a dot with a stem. You'll find it occupying the middle space (staff line 3) of the staff.

- **The Hi-Hat:** Unlike the drums, the hi-hat, a cymbal played with both foot and stick, is represented by an X. The regular hi-hat notation, indicating a closed hi-hat sound played with the foot pedal, sits above the top line (staff line -1) of the staff with a stem pointing downward. The hi-hat pedal notation, for opening and closing the hi-hat with your foot, is an X with a stem positioned below the bottom line (below staff line 8).

- **Open/Closed Hi-Hat Variations:** A small 'o' above the hi-hat symbol indicates an open hi-hat played with the stick, while a small '+' signifies a closed hi-hat. There are additional symbols for more nuanced hi-hat articulations, like a loose hi-hat (ø) and an open/close (o+), which you'll encounter as you progress in your drumming journey.

- **The Ride Cymbal:** The ride cymbal, often used for keeping time and accents, is denoted by an X with a stem placed on the top line (staff line 0) of the staff.

Bass drum   Snare   Floor tom   Middle tom   High tom

18. Drum notation. Source: No machine-readable author provided. Bigbluefish assumed (based on copyright claims)., Public domain, via Wikimedia Commons. https://commons.wikimedia.org/wiki/File:Drumkit_notation_drums.png

This is just a foundational understanding of drum notation. As you explore more complex music, you'll encounter additional symbols and markings that convey dynamics (volume), accents, and other subtleties of drumming.

Setting SMART Goals

As with any endeavor, setting goals is crucial for developing your drumming skills and tracking your progress. However, not just any goal will do.

The most effective goals are SMART goals, meaning they are:

- **Specific:** Clearly define what you want to achieve. Instead of a vague goal like "improve my drumming," aim for something specific like "master the single stroke roll at 60 beats per minute (bpm)."

- **Measurable:** How will you know when you've reached your goal? Make sure your goals have a measurable component. In the drumming example above, being able to play the single-stroke roll cleanly and consistently at 60 bpm is a clear measurement of success.

- **Achievable:** Set challenging but attainable goals. While you aspire to be the next drumming legend, aiming to master a complex paradiddle fill in your first week might be a bit too ambitious. Start with achievable goals and gradually increase the difficulty as you progress.

- **Relevant:** Your goals should be relevant to your overall drumming aspirations. If your dream is to play heavy rock music, practicing rudiments for jazz drumming might not be the most relevant use of your practice time.

- **Time-bound:** Set a timeframe for achieving your goals. This will add a sense of urgency and help you stay motivated. Aim to master that single-stroke roll at 60 bpm within the next two weeks.

Examples of SMART Drumming Goals for Beginners

- Master the single stroke roll at 60 bpm within two weeks.

- Play a basic rock beat (bass drum on beats 1 and 3, hi-hat on eighth notes, snare on beats 2 and 4) with clean coordination at 80 bpm within a month.

- Learn and play along to three beginner-friendly drum fills at slow tempos within three months.

SMART goals are your roadmap to drumming success. They keep you focused and motivated and help you celebrate your achievements along the way.

The Power of Consistent Practice

Just like building muscle requires consistent workouts, developing your drumming skills thrives on regular, focused practice. While the occasional long practice session might seem appealing, cramming weeks' worth of practice into one day is not the most effective approach.

Here's why:

- **Focus and Concentration:** Your ability to focus and concentrate deteriorates over extended periods. Shorter, more frequent practice sessions allow you to maintain a higher level of focus and concentration, leading to more efficient learning.

- **Muscle Memory:** Drumming relies heavily on muscle memory. Shorter practice sessions spread throughout the week allow your muscles to absorb and solidify the techniques you're working on, leading to long-term improvement.

- **Motivation:** Facing a daunting block of practice time is demotivating. Shorter sessions feel more manageable and can help you stay motivated to pick up your sticks and practice consistently.

Aim for shorter, daily practice sessions of 15 to 30 minutes is highly beneficial to maximize your focus, build muscle memory, and keep the drumming fire burning bright.

Your Personalized Path to Progress

If you clearly understand the importance of SMART goals and consistent practice, start building a sample practice routine to get started:

- **Warm-up (5 to 10 minutes):** Start with some light stretches for your arms, wrists, and shoulders to prepare your body for drumming. Then, practice basic strokes (single strokes, double strokes) slowly on a practice pad to get your muscles warmed up and your coordination flowing.

- **Focused Skill Practice (15 to 20 minutes):** This is where you work on your SMART goals. Maybe today's focus is mastering the single-stroke roll. Practice the stroke slowly and deliberately, gradually increasing the tempo as your control improves. Use a metronome to maintain a steady beat. If you're working on a specific beat or rudiment, break it down into smaller sections and practice them individually before putting it all together.

- **Playing Along to Music (10 to 15 minutes):** Make drumming fun. Put on some of your favorite music (use headphones if necessary), and try playing along to the beat. Start with simpler songs and gradually progress to more challenging ones as you improve. This is a great way to apply the skills you're practicing in a musical context and develop your sense of groove.

19. Drum along to music. Source:
https://www.pexels.com/photo/woman-in-white-crew-neck-t-
shirt-wearing-black-sunglasses-4114926/

This is just a sample structure. Feel free to customize your practice routine based on your individual needs, goals, and interests. The most important thing is to find a routine that works for you and that you can stick to consistently. As you progress on your drumming adventure, you can expand your practice routine to include more advanced techniques, explore different styles of drumming, and develop musical creativity.

Chapter 5: Playing Drum Music

Having mastered the fundamentals and conquered basic beats, you're now ready to explore the diverse drumming styles. This chapter uncovers various musical genres, equipping you to express yourself not just as a drummer but as a storyteller wielding the power of rhythm. Get ready to explore the driving force behind rock anthems, the swinging pulse of jazz, the infectious grooves of funk, and so much more.

20. Explore different genres. Source:Designed by freepik.
https://www.freepik.com/free-vector/hand-drawn-
drums_1132754.htm

A Genre Guide

The beauty of drumming lies in its versatility. The techniques you've learned can be applied to a vast array of musical styles, each with its unique rhythmic vocabulary. It's time to explore some of the most popular genres and the essential drumming techniques that make them tick:

- **Rock:** The pounding heart of rock music often relies on powerful beats with a clear backbeat (emphasizing beats 2 and 4). Rock drummers utilize a variety of techniques, such as single and double strokes, accented snare hits, and driving bass drum patterns to create a solid foundation for the music. Subgenres like heavy metal often explore faster tempos and complex fills, while classic rock might feature more laid-back grooves with swing feels.

- **Jazz:** Jazz drumming is a playground for creativity and improvisation. Jazz drummers often employ a lighter touch on the cymbals, utilizing techniques like hi-hat accents, ride cymbal patterns, and delicate snare work to create a swinging feel that complements the improvisational nature of the music. Brush drumming, using brushes instead of sticks, is another hallmark of jazz drumming, adding a softer, subtler texture.

- **Funk:** Get ready to get funky. Funk drumming is all about the groove; the infectious beats that make you want to move. Funk drummers often utilize syncopation (accents on off-beats) and ghost notes (soft snare hits) to create a hypnotic, driving feel. Tight hi-hat patterns and strategically placed bass drum kicks add further depth and rhythmic complexity.

- **Hip-Hop:** In hip-hop, the drumbeat forms the backbone of the track. Hip-hop drumming often relies on programmed beats and samples, but skilled live drummers bring a whole new dimension to the music. They incorporate tight hi-hat patterns, intricate snare work, and creative use of cymbals to create rhythmic textures that perfectly complement the lyrical flow and swagger of hip-hop.

- **Latin Music:** Latin music boasts melodious rhythms. Latin drumming styles like Salsa, Merengue, and Samba utilize complex patterns, often incorporating clave rhythms (specific rhythmic patterns that form the genre's foundation). These styles often involve intricate hi-hat footwork, lively cowbell patterns, and distinctive use of various hand percussion instruments alongside the drum set.

As you explore different genres, pay close attention to the specific techniques used by drummers in those styles. Listen to recordings, watch live performances, and try to emulate the sounds and feels that resonate with you.

Beyond the Technique

Drumming is more than just hitting drums in the right order. It's a powerful tool for expressing emotions and conveying musical ideas. Here are some ways to add expression and nuance to your drumming:

Dynamics

Varying the volume of your hits adds depth and emotion to your playing. Play softer for quieter sections and accentuate important moments with stronger hits.

Here's how to incorporate dynamics:

- **Pianissimo (ppp) to Piano (pp):** This is very soft and quiet playing. Use it for delicate passages or building tension before a big moment.

- **Mezzo Piano (mp):** Medium soft. A good starting point for many grooves and fills.

- **Mezzo Forte (mf):** Medium loud. Adds emphasis to important beats or sections.

- **Forte (f):** Loud. Use this for powerful accents or energetic sections of the music.

- **Fortissimo (ff):** Very loud. Save this for explosive moments that demand maximum impact.

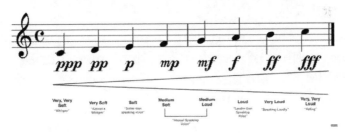

21. Dynamics. Source: jobu0101, CC BY-SA 3.0 <https://creativecommons.org/licenses/by-sa/3.0>, via Wikimedia Commons. https://commons.wikimedia.org/wiki/File:Dynamische_Grundstuf en_edited.png

Experiment with Dynamics. Try playing a simple beat and gradually crescendo (get louder) throughout the phrase. Then, try the opposite by playing a decrescendo (get quieter). Dynamics can completely change the feel of your drumming.

Ghost Notes

Ghost notes are softer snare drum hits that add a whispery sound to your beat. They create a sense of anticipation, build tension, or simply add rhythmic intrigue. They're spices in your drumming recipe. A little goes a long way.

Here's how to play ghost notes:

- Raise your sticks slightly higher than you normally would for a full snare hit.

- Play the snare drum with a loose grip and a lighter touch. Focus on using your fingers more than your whole arm for the stroke.

Ghost notes are all about feel, not volume. Practice playing them slowly with a metronome until you can incorporate them into your drumming vocabulary seamlessly.

Fill Timing

Fills are those short bursts of drumming that bridge between sections of a song or add excitement during a drum solo. While fills are flashy and impressive, it's important to use them strategically to enhance the music, not just show off your chops.

Here are some tips for using fills effectively:

- **Listen to the Music:** Pay attention to the phrasing and structure of the song. Place your fills where they naturally fit the musical flow.

- **Start Simple:** Don't try to cram complex fills into every space. Begin with simple fills that complement the groove, and gradually build your vocabulary as you progress.

- **Leave Space:** Don't fill every silence. Sometimes, a well-placed pause is just as effective as a fancy fill.

Cymbal Choice and Technique

Your drum set offers a variety of cymbals, each with its unique sound and character. Experimenting with different cymbals and techniques allows you to create a wider sonic palette and add color and texture to your drumming.

- **Ride Cymbal:** The ride cymbal is often used for keeping time and playing accents. Crashing the ride cymbal with a forceful hit adds a powerful punctuation mark to the music.

- **Hi-Hat:** Varying your hi-hat technique can create a wide array of sounds. Play closed hi-hats for a tight, crisp sound, open hi-hats for a brighter, airier sound, and experiment with foot splashes on the hi-hat for subtle accents.

- **Other Cymbals:** Crash cymbals are ideal for creating explosive accents and dramatic moments. Splash cymbals add a shimmering, quick burst of sound. Explore the sonic possibilities of your cymbals to expand your drumming vocabulary.

The key to expressive drumming is listening to the music and letting the emotion of the song guide your playing. Feel the rhythm, experiment, and, most importantly, have fun. The next chapter will provide essential tips for drum care and maintenance, ensuring your instrument stays in top condition and delivers the sound you desire for years to come.

Chapter 6: Drum Care and Maintenance

Just like any fine instrument, your drum set deserves proper care and maintenance to keep it sounding its best and lasting for years to come. This chapter equips you with the knowledge to care for your drums, ensuring they're always ready to deliver your rhythmic creations.

22. Your drum set deserves proper care and maintenance to keep it sounding its best and lasting for years to come. Source: https://www.pexels.com/photo/a-room-with-musical-instruments-9644665/

You'll discover essential maintenance routines, proper storage, and handling techniques, and troubleshooting common drum issues you might encounter. By following these simple guidelines, you'll keep your drum set in top condition, allowing you to focus on what truly matters: making music.

Essential Drum Maintenance Tips

Your drum set is your loyal musical companion, faithfully translating your rhythmic ideas into powerful sound. Just like any instrument, proper maintenance ensures your drums function optimally, sound their best, and last for years. This chapter equips you with essential tips to keep your drum kit in top condition.

General Cleaning

- **Dust Regularly:** After each playing session, use a soft, dry cloth to wipe down your drums. This removes dust, sweat, and fingerprints that build up and affect the sound quality. Avoid using harsh chemicals or abrasive cleaners, as they will damage the drum finishes.

- **Cymbal Care:** Cymbals are particularly susceptible to fingerprints and oils from your hands. Invest in a cymbal cleaning cloth specifically designed to remove these elements without harming the cymbal's finish. Avoid using harsh chemicals or abrasive cleaners on your cymbals as well.

Tuning

- **The Importance of Tuning:** Proper tuning is essential for a drum's sound quality and playability.

A well-tuned drum will resonate clearly and project well, while a poorly-tuned drum will sound dull or choked. Tuning drums is a bit tricky at first, but with practice and the right tools (drum key, tuning gauge [optional]), you'll learn to do it yourself. There are also many online resources and tutorials available to guide you through the tuning process.

- **Seek Professional Help:** If you're unsure about tuning your drums, don't hesitate to seek help from a professional drum technician. They will tune your drums perfectly and identify any potential hardware issues that need attention.

Hardware Maintenance

- **Tighten Up:** Over time, the nuts, and bolts on your drum hardware (stands, pedals, hi-hat clutch) become loose. Periodically check all the hardware for tightness and use drum keys to adjust as needed. Loose hardware is frustrating to play with and can also lead to damage if left unaddressed.

- **Oiling the Machine:** The moving parts on your drum pedals and hi-hat clutch rely on proper lubrication to function smoothly and quietly. Use a lubricant specifically designed for drum hardware (avoid WD-40) to keep these parts moving freely and prevent squeaks and other unwanted noises.

Taking a few minutes to care for your drums after each playing session and performing regular maintenance will keep your kit sounding its best for years to come.

Drum Storage and Handling

- **Find a Safe Haven:** When not in use, store your drums in a cool, dry place away from direct sunlight and extreme temperatures. Heat and humidity damage drum finishes and warp the drum shells, affecting their sound and tuning stability. Keep your drums in their original cases if available. These cases are designed to protect the drums from bumps, scratches, and dust.

- **Cover Up:** If you don't have the original cases, invest in high-quality drum bags, or fitted dust covers. These provide a good alternative to cases and will protect your drums from dust and debris while stored.

- **Lifting and Carrying:** Always use proper lifting techniques when moving your drums. Avoid lifting heavy drum pieces by yourself. If possible, call a friend to help you. Use both hands to support the bottom and side of the drum when lifting. For larger drums (bass drum, floor tom), lift from the bottom with your legs and keep your back straight. When carrying drums, hold them securely and avoid bumping them into anything. Consider using drum carriers for easier transport of multiple drums.

- **Hardware Breakdown:** If you need to store your drums for an extended period or transport them over long distances, consider breaking down the drum set partially. Remove the toms from their mounts and store them inside the bass drum for added protection. Detach the cymbals from their stands and store them in cymbal bags or sleeves.

By following these storage and handling guidelines, you'll minimize the risk of damage to your valuable drumming companion.

Troubleshooting Common Drum Problems

Even with the best care, occasional glitches are inevitable with any drum set. Don't fret. Here are some solutions to troubleshoot some common drum problems you might encounter:

The Drum Sounds Dull or Choked

- **Tuning Trouble:** Improper tuning is the most likely culprit for a dull or choked sound. Ensure your drums are tuned correctly using a drum key and a tuning gauge (optional).

- **Head Replacement:** Worn-out drum heads also contribute to a dull sound. If your drum heads have been on your kit for a long time, consider replacing them with fresh heads. New heads will bring back the brightness and resonance of your drums.

Loss of Volume or Sustain

- **Tuning Too Loose:** If your drums lack volume and sustain, they might be tuned too loosely. Tighten the lugs slightly using a drum key, but be careful not to over-tighten.

- **Muffling Issues:** Internal dampening devices (if present on your drums) can sometimes mute the sound. Experiment with adjusting the dampening or removing it completely to see if it improves the volume and sustain.

Hi-Hat Not Closing Properly

- **Clutch Adjustment:** The hi-hat clutch might need adjustment. Consult your hi-hat stand's manual for specific instructions on adjusting the clutch tension.

- **Broken Clutch:** Sometimes, the hi-hat clutch might be worn out or broken. If adjusting the clutch doesn't solve the problem, you might need to replace it.

23. Hit-Hat Clutch. Source: Andrewa, CC BY-SA 3.0 <https://creativecommons.org/licenses/by-sa/3.0>, via Wikimedia Commons. https://commons.wikimedia.org/wiki/File:Hi-hat_clutch_on_a_cymbal.JPG

Squeaks and Rattles from Hardware

- **Tighten Up:** Loose nuts and bolts on your drum hardware cause squeaks and rattles. Use a drum key to tighten all the hardware on your stands and pedals.

- **Lubrication:** The moving parts on your pedals and hi-hat clutch might be dry and require lubrication. Use a drum-specific lubricant to keep these parts moving smoothly and quietly (again, avoid WD-40).

Cracked Drum Shells or Broken Hardware

- **Seek Professional Help:** Cracked drum shells or broken hardware compromise the sound and safety of your drum set. If you encounter such issues, it's best to seek help from a professional drum technician for repairs or replacements.

These are just some of the common drum problems you might face. If you encounter an issue not covered here, consult your drum set's manual or search online resources for specific troubleshooting steps. With a bit of detective work and the tips provided, you'll get your drum set sounding its best in no time. The final chapter of this guide will explore the vast and fascinating drumming history and repertoire, opening a doorway to a wealth of knowledge and inspiration.

Chapter 7: Exploring Drum History and Repertoire

The drum, the heartbeat of countless musical traditions, boasts a rich history that stretches back millennia. More than just a percussion instrument, it's a cultural cornerstone, a powerful voice in storytelling, and a driving force behind countless musical styles. This chapter will teleport you through the history of the drum, exploring its diverse cultural significance, the legendary players who shaped its evolution, and the exciting innovations that continue to push the boundaries of drumming today.

24. The drum, the heartbeat of countless musical traditions, boasts a rich history that stretches back millennia. Source: Gary Todd, CC0, via Wikimedia Commons.
https://commons.wikimedia.org/wiki/File:Lang_Son_Bronze_Drum_a.jpg

The Drum's Cultural and Historical Context

The drum's history stretches back millennia, weaving itself into countless cultures across the globe. It was a powerful tool used for communication, ritual ceremonies, and even warfare. Here's a whirlwind tour of some fascinating examples:

- **Ancient Rhythms:** Archeological evidence suggests drums existed as early as Mesopotamia and the Indus Valley civilization around 5,500 BC. Early drums were likely simple, constructed from animal skins stretched over hollowed logs or clay pots. These early instruments played a role in religious ceremonies and community gatherings.

- **Tribal Communication:** In Africa, often considered the birthplace of drumming, various drum rhythms were a form of communication. Specific beats could relay messages over long distances, warn of danger, announce celebrations, or coordinate hunts.

- **The Call to Battle:** Throughout history, drums have played a vital role in warfare. Their booming sounds intimidated enemies, boosted troop morale, and even coordinated battle formations.

- **Spiritual Connections:** In many cultures, drums held deep spiritual significance. Shamans used them to induce trances and connect with the spirit world. Rhythms were believed to possess healing power or appease deities.

- **Global Influence:** The drum's journey transcended geographical boundaries. Trade routes carried drumming traditions around the world, influencing the development of new styles and techniques. For example, West African drumming traditions had a profound impact on the evolution of drumming in the Americas after European colonization.

As you dive deeper into the following sections of this chapter, you'll explore the stories of specific drummers, famous compositions, and modern innovations that continue to shape the ever-evolving world of drumming. However, the drum's rich cultural and historical context reminds you that rhythm is a powerful language, one that has resonated through time and across cultures, uniting people through the universal beat of the drum.

Iconic Drummers and Their Compositions

The drum throne has been graced by countless phenomenal players who have propelled the instrument forward and left behind an enduring legacy of groundbreaking compositions.

Here are some of these drumming legends and their significant contributions:

- **Gene Krupa (1909-1973):** A pioneer of the jazz drumming style, Krupa was renowned for his technical virtuosity and powerful swing. His composition, "Sing, Sing, Sing" (performed with Benny Goodman), became a cornerstone of big band jazz drumming, showcasing his innovative use of the hi-hat and ride cymbal. Krupa's influence extended beyond jazz, inspiring countless rock drummers with his powerful attack and dynamic sense of phrasing.

- **John Bonham (1948-1980):** The legendary drummer of Led Zeppelin, Bonham's thunderous style and powerful fills redefined rock drumming. His iconic work on tracks like "Moby Dick" and "Stairway to Heaven" continues to inspire drummers worldwide. Bonham wasn't just a powerhouse player; his drumming was infused with incredible feel and musicality. He understood the interplay between drums and other instruments, creating grooves that were as catchy as they were complex.

- **Buddy Rich (1917-1987):** A true showman, Buddy Rich was known for his blazing speed, incredible accuracy, and flamboyant style. While not a prolific composer himself, his virtuosity on the drums left an undeniable mark on the drumming world. Rich pushed the boundaries of what was considered possible on the drum set, inspiring drummers to develop their chops and technique. His influence is still heard in the work of countless drummers across various genres.

25. Buddy Rich. Source: James Kriegsmann, Public domain, via Wikimedia Commons. https://commons.wikimedia.org/wiki/File:Buddy_Rich_1946_pub licity_photo.jpg

- **Bernard Purdie (1939-):** A highly influential session drummer, Purdie's work graced countless soul, funk, and R&B recordings. His signature "Purdie Shuffle" groove, characterized by a ghost note on the snare before the beat, is a staple in many genres of music. More than about technical ability, Purdie's drumming was about creating deep pockets and infectious grooves that laid down the foundation for the entire song. His ability to craft feels that were both sophisticated and danceable made him a highly sought-after session drummer.

- **Neil Peart (1952-2020):** The late Neil Peart, drummer for the progressive rock band Rush, was revered for his technical proficiency, complex compositions, and integration of electronic drums into his kit. His work on songs like "YYZ" and "Tom Sawyer" pushed the boundaries of drumming in rock music. Peart was a musician who thought conceptually about his craft. His compositions incorporated elements of polyrhythms, odd time signatures, and dynamic changes, challenging drummers to expand their vocabulary and approach the instrument in new ways.

Compositions that Shaped Drumming

These are just a few examples of the many drummers who have shaped the history of drumming. Their iconic compositions continue to be benchmarks for aspiring drummers and a testament to the power and artistry of drumming:

- **"Caravan," by Duke Ellington (1936):** Featuring a driving beat by drummer Sonny Greer, "Caravan" is a classic example of swing drumming in big band jazz. Greer's precise and energetic performance perfectly complements the playful melody and horn sections, creating a timeless jazz masterpiece.

- **"Good Times, Bad Times," by Led Zeppelin (1969):** John Bonham's powerful drumming on this track, particularly the iconic intro, is a masterclass in rock drumming. His use of dynamics and fills creates a sense of anticipation and excitement that perfectly sets the stage for the rest of the song. Bonham's drumming on "Good Times, Bad Times" is a prime example of how drumming can elevate a song from good to great.

- **"Impressions," by John Coltrane (1961):** Elvin Jones' innovative drumming on this modal jazz masterpiece showcases his polyrhythmic approach and use of space. Jones' unconventional drumming challenged the traditional role of the drummer in jazz, creating a more interactive and textural soundscape. His work on "Impressions" continues to inspire drummers to explore new rhythmic concepts and push the boundaries of their creativity.

- **"Back in Black," by AC/DC (1980):** Phil Rudd's simple yet effective drumming on this track perfectly complements the song's raw energy and remains a staple of hard rock drumming. Rudd's stripped-down approach demonstrates the power of a solid backbeat and groove in rock music. His drumming on "Back in Black" is a masterclass in "less is more." It proves that intricate drumming isn't always necessary to create a powerful and impactful performance.

26. "Back in Black," by AC/DC. Source: Doctoracdc72, CC BY-SA 3.0 <https://creativecommons.org/licenses/by-sa/3.0>, via Wikimedia Commons.
https://commons.wikimedia.org/wiki/File:ACDC_Tacoma.jpg

This brief exploration highlights just a handful of the many drummers and compositions that have left an indelible mark on the drumming landscape. As you continue your drumming journey, dive deeper into the work of these and other drumming greats. Listen actively, analyze their techniques, and try to incorporate elements of their styles into your playing. There's always something new to learn, a new groove to discover, and a new legend to inspire you.

Modern Developments and Innovations in Drumming

The drum set, as you know it today, is a culmination of centuries of evolution. Modern drumming continues to push boundaries, thanks to constant innovation in technology, materials, and playing styles. It's time to explore some of the exciting developments shaping the drumming landscape:

- **Electronic Drumming Advancements:** The rise of electronic drums has revolutionized drumming in numerous ways. Modern electronic kits offer a vast array of high-quality, sampled sounds, allowing drummers to explore genres and styles that might be outside the reach of traditional acoustic drums. Electronic drums also excel in live settings, offering greater control over volume and the ability to trigger samples and effects. Advancements in responsiveness make electronic kits much more natural to play compared to earlier models.

- **Drumming Software and Apps:** Technology has become a valuable tool for drummers of all levels. Drumming software and apps offer a wealth of learning resources, interactive lessons, and practice tools. These are particularly helpful for beginners, providing feedback on timing and accuracy and offering a fun and engaging way to learn essential drumming skills. For experienced players, drumming software can be used to compose drum tracks, experiment with electronic sounds, and even practice with virtual bands.

- **Hybrid Drumming Setups:** Many drummers are embracing hybrid setups that combine acoustic and electronic elements. This allows them to leverage the classic sound and feel of acoustic drums with the versatility and sonic possibilities of electronic drums. Triggering systems allow drummers to convert the acoustic sound of their drums into electronic sounds, opening doors to creative sound design and integration with electronic music production.

- **Advanced Drum Manufacturing:** Drum manufacturers are constantly exploring new materials and techniques to enhance the sound quality, durability, and playability of drums. Shells are being constructed from innovative wood plies, synthetic materials, and even acrylics, each offering unique tonal characteristics. Heads are being developed with advanced coatings and materials to provide greater responsiveness, durability, and a wider range of sounds. The focus on ergonomics and comfort is also leading to improvements in drum thrones, hardware, and sticks, allowing drummers to play for longer periods without fatigue.

- **The Evolving Drummer:** Modern drumming is all about creativity, expression, and pushing boundaries. Drummers are increasingly incorporating elements from various genres into their playing, creating unique hybrid styles. There's also a growing emphasis on musicality, where drummers are seen as integral storytellers within a band, not just timekeepers.

The future of drumming is brimming with exciting possibilities. With continued technological advancements, innovative materials, and a generation of endlessly creative drummers, the rhythmic landscape will undoubtedly continue to evolve and surprise you. As you explore the nuances of drumming, remember that you're becoming part of an ever-evolving tradition. Embrace the innovations, explore the rich history, and most importantly, have fun expressing yourself through the power of the rhythm.

Conclusion

You've reached the final beat of "Drums for Kids," and you're now equipped for a thrilling drumming adventure. This book has been your guide, introducing you to the fascinating drums, from the fundamental components of a drum set to essential playing techniques and the rich history of this powerful instrument.

As you turn the final page, revisit some of the key takeaways to fuel your drumming journey:

Key Takeaways

- **Meet Your Musical Companion:** You've become familiar with the essential parts of a drum set, from the deep boom of the bass drum to the bright crash of the cymbals. Now, you can identify each component and understand its role in creating the rhythmic foundation of music.

- **A Solid Start:** Setting up your drum set correctly and maintaining proper posture are the building blocks for comfortable and effective playing. With a well-positioned kit and good posture, you'll be ready to tackle any beat with confidence.

- **Mastering the Fundamentals:** You've discovered essential drumming techniques, such as holding the sticks correctly, mastering basic strokes (single stroke, double stroke), and coordinating your hands and feet. These skills are the foundation upon which you'll build your drumming vocabulary and explore more complex rhythms.

- **Building Your Skills:** Through engaging exercises and practice routines, you've developed your coordination, timing, and overall drumming prowess. Consistent practice is key to improvement. The more you play, the more comfortable and confident you'll become behind the drum set.

- **Unlocking the Language of Drums:** You've been introduced to basic drum notation, allowing you to decipher written drum parts and play along to your favorite songs. This opens the door to a vast library of drumming possibilities and the ability to collaborate with other musicians.

- **Taking Care of Your Kit:** Proper cleaning, maintenance, and storage will ensure your drum set sounds its best for years to come. Taking good care of your instrument is an essential part of being a responsible drummer.

- **A Journey Through Rhythm:** You've embarked on a captivating exploration of drumming history, uncovering its cultural significance across the globe and meeting legendary drummers who have shaped the way we play today. This rich history provides context and appreciation for the instrument you're learning to master.

These are just the initial beats of your drumming adventure. As you continue to practice, explore different styles of music, and experiment with new techniques, remember that drumming is a lifelong experience filled with discovery and endless possibilities. Keep these key takeaways in mind as you push your boundaries, express yourself through rhythm, and find your unique drumming voice.

If you enjoyed your drumming exploration with "Drums for Kids," leave a review and share your drumming experience. Include what you liked about the book, what new drumming skills you learned, and what kind of drumming adventures you're excited about embarking on. Keep drumming and keep on rocking. The world needs to hear your rhythm.

References

Drum Notation & Sheet Music: How to Read It - Drum Beats Online. (n.d.). Drumbeatsonline.com. https://drumbeatsonline.com/blog/drum-notation-sheet-music-how-to-read-it

Flumpkins. (2019, April 9). Learn the Drumming Basics! Instructables. https://www.instructables.com/How-to-play-drums/

How to Play Drums: The Complete Guide for Beginners. (2023, June 9). Takelessons.com. https://takelessons.com/blog/how-to-play-drums-the-complete-guide-for-beginners

KITCHIN, J. (2019, November 7). How To Read & Write Drum Sheet Music (Drum Notation Guide). Beatsure. https://beatsure.com/drum-sheet-music/

Kitchin, J. (2019, October 29). How To Play Drums For Beginners (Learning Online Made EASY). Beatsure. https://beatsure.com/how-to-play-drums/

Landa, S. (2019, December 2). How To Play Drums: The Ultimate Resource For Beginner Drummers. The Beat. https://www.drumeo.com/beat/how-to-play-drums/

Moss, C. (2022, March 21). What Do I Need to Play Drums? Notes for New Drummers. Roland Articles. https://articles.roland.com/what-do-i-need-to-play-drums-notes-for-new-drummers/

Nick_S_c_h_l_e_singer. (2016, April 6). An Easy Guide To Learning and Playing Drums By Ear. Nick Schlesinger. https://nickschlesinger.com/playing-drums-by-ear

Stein, T. (2023, January 23). How To Play Drums: Get Started Learning Drums Today. Music Careers | Expert Advice - Careers in Music. https://www.careersinmusic.com/how-to-play-drums/

65622799R00049